D1604874

INTO THE
WORLD'S
AMAZING
JUNGLES

JUNGLE BUGS
& VEGETATION

LORI VETERE

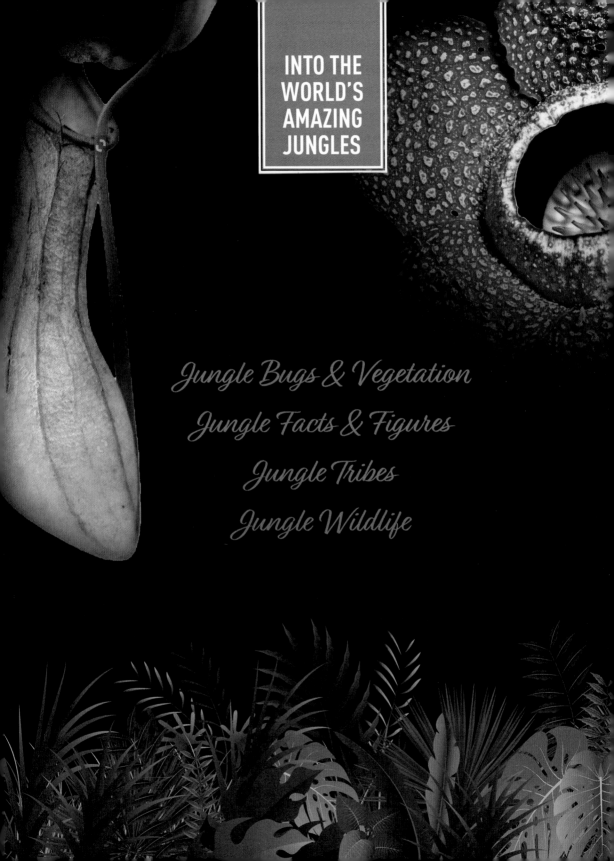

INTO THE WORLD'S AMAZING JUNGLES

Jungle Bugs & Vegetation

Jungle Facts & Figures

Jungle Tribes

Jungle Wildlife

INTO THE
WORLD'S
AMAZING
JUNGLES

JUNGLE BUGS
& VEGETATION

LORI VETERE

MC

MASON CREST

Mason Crest
450 Parkway Drive, Suite D
Broomall, Pennsylvania 19008
(866) MCP-BOOK (toll-free)
www.masoncrest.com

First printing
9 8 7 6 5 4 3 2 1

ISBN (hardback) 978-1-4222-4094-6
ISBN (series) 978-1-4222-4092-2
ISBN (ebook) 978-1-4222-7703-4

Library of Congress Cataloging-in-Publication Data

    Names: Vetere, Lori, author.
    Title: Jungle bugs & vegetation / Lori Vetere.
    Other titles: Jungle bugs and vegetation
    Description: Broomall, Philadelphia : Mason Crest, [2019] | Series: Into the
      world's amazing jungles | Includes bibliographical references and index.
    Identifiers: LCCN 2018004082 (print) | LCCN 2018008513 (ebook) | ISBN
      9781422277034 (eBook) | ISBN 9781422240946 (hardcover) | ISBN
      9781422240922 (series)
    Subjects: LCSH: Jungle plants. | Rain forest plants. | Jungle animals. |
      Insects. | Jungle ecology.
    Classification: LCC SB434.5 (ebook) | LCC SB434.5 .V48 2019 (print) | DDC
      635.9/523--dc23
    LC record available at https://lccn.loc.gov/2018004082

Developed and Produced by National Highlights Inc.
Editor: Andrew Luke
Interior and cover design: Jana Rade, impact studios
Production: Michelle Luke

CONTENTS

KEY ICONS TO LOOK FOR:

 Words to Understand: These words with their easy-to-understand definitions will increase the reader's understanding of the text while building vocabulary skills.

 Sidebars: This boxed material within the main text allows readers to build knowledge, gain insights, explore possibilities, and broaden their perspectives by weaving together additional information to provide realistic and holistic perspectives.

 Educational Videos: Readers can view videos by scanning our QR codes, providing them with additional educational content to supplement the text. Examples include news coverage, moments in history, speeches, iconic sports moments, and much more!

 Text-Dependent Questions: These questions send the reader back to the text for more careful attention to the evidence presented there.

 Research Projects: Readers are pointed toward areas of further inquiry connected to each chapter. Suggestions are provided for projects that encourage deeper research and analysis.

 Series Glossary of Key Terms: This back-of-the book glossary contains terminology used throughout this series. Words found here increase the reader's ability to read and comprehend higher-level books and articles in this field.

THE CONGO

Area – 687,000 m^2 (1,780,000 km^2).

Home to: Aka tribes, Forest Leopards, Raffia Palms.

This jungle is the basin of the Congo river, covering the northern half of the Democratic Republic of the Congo and spreading west toward the Atlantic Ocean through five other countries.

More than 400 species of mammals, 700 species of fish, and 1,000 species of birds are found here.

THE AMAZON

Area – 2,123,000 m^2 (5,500,000 km^2).

Home to: Tribes of Acre, Giant Otters, Rubber trees.

About half of the world's biggest jungle is located in Brazil. The other half spreads into eight other South American countries.

The Amazon contains 20% of all the freshwater in the world.

SUNDARBANS RESERVE

Area – 4000 m^2 (10,000 km^2).

Home to: Bengal Tigers.

This region lies mostly in Bangladesh and spreads to the west into India.

The Sundarbans was declared a UNESCO World Heritage Site in 1997.

PAPUA NEW GUINEA

Area – 116,000 m^2 (300,000 km^2).

Home to: Huli tribes, Tree Kangaroos, Blue Marble trees.

The eastern half of the island of New Guinea is the country known as Papua New Guinea and was once almost completely covered by jungle. Since 1972, more than 80,000 km^2, or more than 20 percent, has been cleared.

BORNEO LOWLAND

Area – 165,000 m^2 (427,500 km2).

Home to: Penan tribes, Proboscis Monkeys, Asian Tiger Mosquitos.

This jungle encompasses the entire island of Borneo, which is shared by Brunei, Malaysia and Indonesia,

In Borneo, 700 tree species were once discovered in just 25 acres (0.1 km^2).

INTRODUCTION

J ungles are living and vibrant parts of our world. Every place you look, you will see something fascinating and beautiful growing, flying, crawling, or walking across the rainforest floor. This book will explore some of the most interesting, exotic, and deadly insects and plants found anywhere on earth. The four largest remaining jungles of the world, which are located in Sarawak, Borneo, the Amazon River Basin, West Central Africa, and Papua New Guinea, are incredible assets to the health and welfare of our planet.

Borneo's jungles are in danger of becoming extinct in the next century. The main cause of its destruction is the logging and corporations that are cutting down the jungle to grow trees in palm oil plantations. Palm oil, which is squeezed from oil palm tree nuts, is used in many household products around the world. Due to this practice, the jungles lose not only trees, but also the habitat for insects, arachnids and plants not found anywhere else in the world.

The Amazon Jungle is also battling against logging activities, deforestation, and bulldozing to promote large-scale agriculture, cattle ranching, mining, large

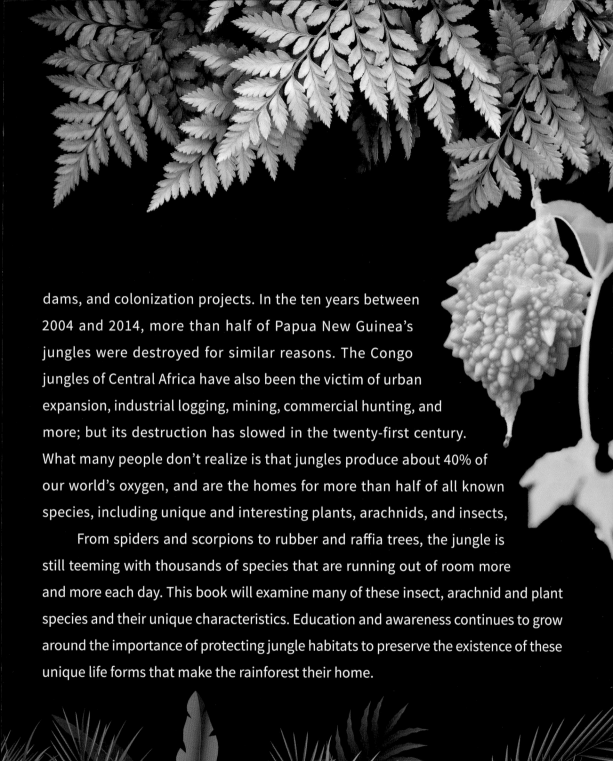

dams, and colonization projects. In the ten years between 2004 and 2014, more than half of Papua New Guinea's jungles were destroyed for similar reasons. The Congo jungles of Central Africa have also been the victim of urban expansion, industrial logging, mining, commercial hunting, and more; but its destruction has slowed in the twenty-first century. What many people don't realize is that jungles produce about 40% of our world's oxygen, and are the homes for more than half of all known species, including unique and interesting plants, arachnids, and insects,

From spiders and scorpions to rubber and raffia trees, the jungle is still teeming with thousands of species that are running out of room more and more each day. This book will examine many of these insect, arachnid and plant species and their unique characteristics. Education and awareness continues to grow around the importance of protecting jungle habitats to preserve the existence of these unique life forms that make the rainforest their home.

WORDS TO UNDERSTAND

latex – a milky fluid or juice which is collected from many plants because of its special rubber properties

parasitic – an organism which lives either in (or on) another organism, gaining protection and nourishment while giving nothing back in return

stigma – a flower pistil's upper part which receives pollen, and where the pollen grain germinates

tendrils – threadlike, leafless organs of climbing plants, often growing in spiral form, which attach to or twines around some other body, so as to support the plant

vulcanization – the process of chemically treating crude rubber in order to give it highly useful properties like strength, stability, and elasticity

Unique Vegetation and Trees

Amazon Jungle Plants and Trees

Rubber trees were unique to the Amazonian rainforest before they were illegally smuggled into Southeast Asia. Their place in history started in 1839 when the process of **vulcanization** was discovered. Yellow or white **latex** is tapped from the trees to make rubber, which is highly prized throughout the world for making tires, rubber hoses, bouncing balls, shoe soles, erasers, toys, hockey pucks, and so much more!

CACAO PLANTS

Raw cacao is one of the main ingredients of chocolate, and it provides natural energy and mental alertness in addition to its wonderful taste. Cacao, from which cocoa is made, contains more calcium than the milk of a cow and more iron than any other

This is how chocolate starts – from a raw cacao plant in the Amazon basin.

plant in existence. The word chocolate comes from the word "xocolatl," a word used by Mayan people meaning "bitter water." The Mayans started making a drink comprised of water, crushed cacao beans, and chili peppers around 900 B.C. They loved it for its energy-giving properties and even called it "food of the gods" (imagine how much more they liked it once sugar was introduced to Central America)!

JABUTICABA

Jabuticaba is an exotic fruit that grows only in the Amazonian jungle of Brazil. It tastes like a slippery-skinned grape but actually looks like a horde of beetles invading the tree it grows on. Its fruit is used to make tarts, jams, strong wines, and even liqueurs. Its sun-dried skin can be used to treat asthma, diarrhea, and as a gargle for inflamed tonsils. Several anti-cancer compounds have been discovered in this fruit.

BRAZIL NUT TREE

The Brazil nut tree is the largest tree growing in the Amazon Jungle and can grow to heights of 160 feet (48.7 meters). Brazil nuts grow inside fruits that weigh 5 pounds and are shaped like baseballs. The fruit's outer layer is so tough that only large rodents called agoutis, which have extremely sharp teeth, are able to crack it open.

GIANT WATER LILIES

Giant water lilies (Victoria amazonica) were discovered in 1801. The circular leaves of this plant are so large that a child weighing up to 99 pounds (45 kilograms) can sit in the center of it! These plants grow in the backwaters of the Amazon River basin. The flowers of this plant only live about forty-eight hours. On the first night the

The pad of a giant water lily can easily support the weight of a large child.

flower opens, it attracts beetles with its sweet pineapple-like odor. The beetles enter the plant and transfer pollen to the **stigma,** fertilizing it. This event occurs over a one-day period while the flower shuts and traps the beetles inside it. The very next day the giant water lily changes color (from white to purplish red) and changes from a female to a male! It opens up on the second evening after changing color and no longer emits a pineapple-like scent. The beetle leaves the plant covered with new pollen and flies off to enter another white flower to repeat the process all over again. At the end of forty-eight hours, the flower closes and sinks down below the water's surface.

Borneo Rainforest Plants and Trees

The largest forested landmass in Asia is thought to be about 130 million years old (even older than the Amazon Jungle). There are an estimated three thousand tree species and more than fifteen thousand species of flowering plants, many of which are unique, in the jungles of Borneo.

Vanilla

Did you know that vanilla originally came from orchids that grew in the jungles of Mexico and Guatemala? The vanilla orchid grows on a 30-foot (9.14 meters) vine that climbs up trees. The part that is used to make vanilla is the pod, or bean, which is opened and scraped to collect thousands of tiny black seeds. These beans are then mashed and mixed with alcohol and water to make vanilla extract. Because this process is expensive, most people today use imitation vanilla flavoring. But imitation flavor will never compare to the sweet-scented pods that helped vanilla win its place as the world's most popular flavor!

TITAN ARUM, THE CORPSE FLOWER

The flowering plant titan arum (Amorphophallus titanum), which grows in the Sarawak jungle, has become famous for its horrible odor which people compare to the odor of a rotting carcass! This plant produces a single cluster of flowers that frequently grow to more than 10 feet (3 meters) in height. Botanical gardens around the world have imported these plants since 1889, and they have contests to see which botanist can grow the tallest plant. The current winner is Louis Ricciardiello, who grew a 10-foot-2-inch (3.1 meters) specimen in 2010 at Winnipesaukee Orchids in New Hampshire.

The corpse flower earned its name for its foul stench, which smells like rotting flesh.

The public is invited to the smelly experience that is the corpse flower at the US Botanic Garden in Washington, D.C.

The other unique thing about this plant is how long it takes to bloom for the first time—seven to ten years—and then arbitrarily it will bloom again either every seven years or every two to six years. The bloom will start to open around mid-afternoon, stay open all through the night, and begin to wilt within twelve hours. That's right—it blooms an incredibly stinky flower only once every seven years or so that lasts for just one night! This flower's unique stench serves to attract insects to it that usually either lay their eggs on top of rotting meat or feed on dead animal corpses. The flesh flies and carrion beetles it attracts will then serve as pollinators of the plant.

Scientists have done an analysis of this plant's "special" smell. The combination of odors that it has been compared to are Limburger cheese, sweaty socks, rotting fish, a sweet floral scent, and a smell similar to human feces!

THE STRANGLER FIG, A TREE KILLER

Imagine, if you will, a fruit-eating animal, like a squirrel or bird, pooping the seeds of the strangler fig onto a tree. The seed will start to germinate; and when it does, it will suck nutrients from the tree and grow to become a **parasitic** tree. The parasitic tree will grow, and its branches will spread from the original tree's crown down to the ground where the roots of both trees will join and make an interlacing basketwork of roots all around the trunk. Finally, since the roots of the strangler fig tree grow faster and thicker, they will constrict nutrient flow into the original tree which will then die.

Strangler fig trees act like parasites, sucking nutrients from the host tree.

Unusual Plants of The Congo Jungle River Basin

LIANAS

Lianas, which are a kind of climbing vine, grow throughout the Congo jungle. Some lianas can grow as long as 3,000 feet (914 meters) long! These plants have sucker roots and **tendrils** that let them attach to trees. They grow rapidly up a tree to get to the area with the most sunlight. Their stems are woody and thick, and they provide a rapid way of transportation for primates living in the jungle.

RAFFIA PALMS

Raffia palms are native to the African jungle, and the fiber of these palms is located on the underside of each frond. This strong, rope-like substance is exported around the world. It is used primarily to make rope, twine, baskets, hats, placemats, textiles,

RESEARCH PROJECT

There are many good videos on YouTube discussing unusual and unique plants and trees of the world's rainforests. Choose a jungle—the Amazon River basin; the Congo River basin; the rainforest of Sarawak, Borneo; or the rainforest of Papua New Guinea—and choose two plants or species of plants that interest you. Write a two-page report on this topic.

and shoes. Raffia fibers are also used locally in construction to provide supporting beams, sticks, and roof coverings.

Another significant use of raffia palm is in the creation of a special cultural drink from its sap that is most popular in Nigeria. Its sap contains sugars that are collected by cutting a box into the top of the palm and suspending a large gourd underneath which collects the tree's milky white liquid. This liquid is then fermented and called wine. It can also be used to create a strong liquor called Ogogoro. Unfortunately, this process kills the raffia palm.

Sapodilla

The sapodilla tree grows in the jungles of Central America. Its bark contains a gummy white sap known as chicle, which was used to create the very first chewing gum by the Aztecs and the Mayans. The fruit of this tree is egg-shaped and tastes somewhat like a pear. Central Americans consider the sapodilla to be the finest tasting fruit around, and the howler monkeys of the rainforest would agree with that opinion!

Unusual Plants of Papua New Guinea

The jungles of Papua New Guinea are more temperate and have richer soils at a higher altitude than other rainforests, results of intense volcanic activity in the region about two hundred thousand years ago. This combination gave birth to many plants that are not found anywhere else on Earth and include more than four thousand fern and orchid species.

Blue marble trees can grow to heights of more than 160 feet.

BLUE MARBLE TREE

This tree, which bears bitter but edible blue fruit, is also known as a blue quandong or a blue fig tree (although it's not related to figs). This tall tree (it can grow to 164 feet (150 meter) bears a round, blue fruit containing a spiraled nut inside. Spectacled flying foxes (also called spectacled fruit bats), woompoo pigeons (also called woompoo fruit doves), and flightless birds called cassowaries eat this fruit whole and then pass the nut undamaged.

MUSA INGENS

Musa ingens happens to be the Earth's tallest banana tree, as well as its biggest herbaceous plant (a plant having almost no woody tissue and usually only existing for one growing season). This plant, which grows best in tropical highland jungles, can grow 49 feet (15 meters) tall and its leaves can be 16 feet (5 meters) long and 3.3 feet (1 meters) wide! Unfortunately, this species is considered wild and its fruit is not edible.

FICUS DAMMAROPSIS

Also known as the highland breadfruit, the Ficus dammaropsis is a large tropical fig tree native to the highland fringe of Papua New Guinea's jungle. This plant has enormous pleated leaves that are 1.9 feet (60 centimeters) wide. The leaves are often used locally as a side dish. They are pickled or cooked as an accompanying vegetable to pig meat. The fruit it produces is edible but not desirable and is eaten only as a last resort.

Epiphytes

Epiphytes are plants that grow on trees and don't need soil to grow. Ferns, orchids, and bromeliads are examples of epiphytes. They are pollinated and spread by certain kinds of birds and insects. Some ferns can grow to be 14 feet tall without ever touching the ground!

TEXT-DEPENDENT QUESTIONS

1. What are some of the different scents that make up the bad smell of the corpse flower?
2. What types of drinks are made from the raffia palm?
3. What is an epiphyte?

WORDS TO UNDERSTAND

alkaloids – a group of bitter-tasting, nitrogen-containing plants that have strong physical effects on humans

fermentation – a process by which change occurs chemically due to reaction with yeasts, bacteria, and other microorganisms, usually via heat, and which causes sugars in plants to be changed into ethyl alcohol

hallucinogenic – causing hallucinations or changes in emotion, thoughts, and consciousness

tachycardia – an abnormally fast heart rate, usually 100+ beats per minute in a resting state

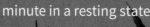

CHAPTER 2

Pretty Poison

Poisonous Plants of The Amazon

Jungles around the world are noted for their amazing and beautiful trees and plants. In addition to being beautiful, a surprising number of plant species are also extremely poisonous. The Amazonian rain forest is a leader in this respect. Indigenous people have used these plants for medicinal, hunting, and ritual purposes for thousands of years.

ANGEL TRUMPET TREE

The flowers of the angel trumpet tree (Brugmansia) have been used by Amazonian medicine men for millennia. The beautiful yellowish-white blooms can grow to be almost a foot long and hang down from the tree. They remind many people of a trumpet that might be played by an angel. When consumed, these flowers have a highly **hallucinogenic** effect. All other parts of this tree are toxic to humans. They were used by indigenous tribes in South America who mix them with tobacco leaves and maize (corn) beer to

Amazonian tribes have used darts dipped in curare-based poison for centuries.

drug unfortunate slaves and wives before they were thrown alive into the tombs of their dead masters. Eating any portion of this shrub can cause confusion, paralysis, dry mouth, **tachycardia**, diarrhea, migraine headaches, auditory and visual hallucinations, and death. Perhaps it's not such a bad thing that this tree is said to be almost extinct in the wild.

CURARE

Curare is the name of a large, poisonous vine that is brimming with **alkaloids**. It has been used for centuries as a source of poison to dip arrows and blowgun darts into before firing them from blowpipes. This poison brings down its target by shutting down the victim's respiratory system and paralyzing them.

A person or animal shot with a curare-dipped arrow will remain conscious while they suffocate to death. When used in small doses, there are other medicinal uses of curare that don't cause immediate death. Curare is harmless if it is eaten. It only becomes poisonous if it is injected directly into its prey by a poisoned arrow or dart.

MANZANILLA DE LA MUERTE (LITTLE APPLE OF DEATH)

Black-Sap Poisonwood or Chechém

In the jungles of Central America and southern Mexico, a tree called black-sap poisonwood grows and contains urushiol (the chemical agent of poison ivy) in its leaves and bark. Anyone that touches the plant usually develops a blistering and painful skin rash.

This beautiful South American tree found in the Amazon Jungle is known as the manchineel, in English, or the manzanilla de la muerte in Spanish, which means "little apple of death." Everything about this tree is poisonous to animals and humans. When it rains, this tree oozes a whitish sap; and if it gets on your skin, it will start blistering. If the tree is burned, it releases incredibly toxic fumes that cause respiratory problems and even blindness whenever humans breathe in the smoke. Eating the fruit of this tree is usually fatal, and according to the many stories about it, whoever eats this little apple suffers a slow and agonizing death.

CALADIUM

Every part of this beautiful-looking plant is poisonous. Known commonly as "heart of Jesus," "elephant ear," or "angel wings," caladium can cause skin irritation with just a touch of these red, pink, and white arrowhead- or heart-shaped leaves; eating any part may cause a serious illness. Most commonly found in Brazil, its leaves are covered with tiny crystallized needles that, if consumed, can cut your insides while making their way through your body. Less poisonous species of this plant are so attractive that they are grown as an ornamental plant in many parts of the world. Cat and dog owners are warned that eating any part of this plant can be deadly to both animals.

The leaves of the caladium plant are distinctly shaped and brightly colored, giving humans plenty of warning to stay away.

Poisonous Plants of Papua New Guinea

GYMPIE GYMPIE PLANT (GIANT STINGING TREE)

If you ever travel to the jungles of Papua New Guinea, there is one plant that you should try to avoid at all costs: the gympie gympie plant. Also known as stinging bush, mulberry-leaved stinger, or moonlighter, this pretty shrub with large heart-shaped leaves and saw-toothed edges does not look dangerous at all. But beware of brushing up against it! You'll get big welts and intense pain wherever you touch it; and chances are you won't be able to stop screaming.

Learn about the dangers of the Giant Stinging Tree.

Ray Mears Demonstrations - Giant Stinging Tree

This shrub has a reputation for killing any animal that happens to touch it. It is so deadly, in fact, that the British did a thorough investigation of it for possible use as a chemical warfare agent. This plant has tiny hairs that implant themselves in your skin and keep exuding its painful chemical for weeks. Victims have described its sting as like being electrocuted and burned with acid at the very same time.

With its telltale heart-shaped leaves, the gympie gympie plant is one of the most venomous plants in the world.

Plants to Avoid in the Jungle

If you want to survive in a jungle, follow these rules about which plants to avoid:

- Stay away from plants that have either yellow or white berries, smell like almonds, have umbrella-shaped flowers, have shiny leaves, or have leaves that are grouped in threes.
- Avoid any beans or plants that have seeds located inside a pod.
- Do not touch anything that has a discolored or milky sap.
- Spit out anything that tastes at all soapy or bitter!

If you are starving and must eat something, you can perform the "universal edibility test" to find out whether a plant can be eaten. Take the plant in question and check it for insects or worms. You'll want a good fresh plant for your test.

1. Select a portion of the plant to test. There are five possible parts of any plant that are edible—the root, stem, buds, flowers, and leaves.

MILKY MANGROVE

The milky mangrove is a small widespread shrub that grows throughout Papua New Guinea. Every part of this plant is poisonous. When it is freshly cut, a bitter poisonous juice that causes blisters on human skin leaks out; it can even cause blindness if it gets into your eyes. Some people have managed to collect this juice to use as a poison to kill fish. Also, if you place some of its crushed leaves into the water, it will daze the fish and cause them to float upward to the water's surface.

2. Crush the piece of the plant you've selected and rub it inside an elbow or wrist for fifteen minutes.
3. Wait eight hours! If you experience any redness, burning sensation, bumps, or welts, you cannot eat it.
4. If you don't have a way to boil the plant, take a piece and hold it against your lips for about five minutes. If you feel tingling or burning, discard that part and try another piece of the plant.
5. Take the same plant part and place it on your tongue. Wait another fifteen minutes. If you feel any tingling or burning, spit it out and wash out your mouth with water.
6. Chew the piece of plant and hold it inside your mouth for fifteen minutes. Do not swallow! Spit it out and rinse with water if you experience anything unusual.
7. Wait another eight hours! If you start to feel nauseous, drink lots of water and make yourself vomit if you can. If you survive the eight hours without any problem, you can chew and eat one-quarter of a cup of the same part of the plant you've been testing.

The milky mangrove is bad news for humans. Its sap causes severe skin blistering and possible blindness if it contacts the eyes.

PANGIUM EDULE (KELUAK OR KEPAYANG)

Pangium edule is a taller tree native to the mangrove swamps of Papua New Guinea. It generates large poisonous fruits called "football fruits," which is edible only after **fermentation**. The seeds and fruit of this tree contain hydrogen cyanide, which is extremely poisonous if eaten without proper treatment.

The seeds must be boiled, and then buried in banana leaves, ash, and soil for approximately 40 days. This process ensures that the poison, which is water-soluble, washes out of the seeds, and it can then be used to make thick cooking gravy.

Bowenia Fern

The Bowenia fern (it is actually more of a palm-like plant) is one of the most toxic plants in the Australian rainforest. Its shiny leaves look like they're made of plastic and are extremely poisonous. It is ironic that this plant is an office favorite throughout the world!

Although edule seeds are initially poisonous, they can be boiled and buried so the poison leeches out.

Poisonous Plants of Borneo

ANTIARIS TOXICARIA OR UPAS TREE

The Penan tribe of Sarawak, Borneo, has hunted with blowpipes and poison-tipped darts for generations, especially if they are hunting smaller prey. This cenuturies-old method traditionally includes using poison sap that comes from the Antiaris toxicaria on the tips of their darts because it can kill an animal without contaminating the meat.

The Antiaris toxicaria is a member of the breadfruit and mulberry families. This tree creates a toxic agent called antiarin. The Penan people cut deep notches into this tree's bark and collect the yellow latex that pours out in a small bamboo container. They then cook the sap slowly over a small fire for approximately one week. Finally, they dip the tips of their darts into the toxic paste. This poison lasts for years and can still be found on darts that have been displayed in museums for many decades.

Antiaris toxicaria, also known as the "arrow-poison tree," is an endangered species. Its milky juice is highly toxic and was used by the Penan to poison their blow darts.

BUAH KELUAK

The buah keluak is a tree native to Borneo, Malaysia, and Indonesia, and its seeds are used in cooking, even though they must be soaked and cooked for hours to get rid of the poisonous hydrocyanic acid inside them. The words "buah keluak" translate to "the fruit that nauseates." One method used to leech the nuts of their poison is to bury seeds that have already been boiled for an entire day with ashes in a pit. The seeds ferment slowly for forty days, reducing the poisonous effect of the hydrocyanic acid.

Poisonous Plants of The African Rainforest

WILD CUCUMBER

The wild cucumber (also called balsam apple) is a vine with dark green leaves native to tropical Africa. This plant bears red-skinned fruit with seeds and pulp that look very much like a cucumber, but both seeds and fruit skin are toxic. Eating it will cause diarrhea and extreme indegestion.

Balsam apple (or wild cucumber) turns from dark green to red when it ripens. It is harmful to humans in either stage.

RESEARCH PROJECT

Do some research on one of the three ways poisonous plants can enter your system—by touching them (skin absorption), by eating them (ingestion), or by breathing in their toxin (inhalation). Write a paper explaining the method you chose and how it works in the body. Then choose a jungle plant that can enter your body through this method and find out what can be done (if anything) to stop the effects of the poison.

TEXT-DEPENDENT QUESTIONS

1. What effect do the flowers of the angel trumpet tree have on humans if consumed?
2. Where does the milky mangrove grow?
3. What is another name for wild cucumber?

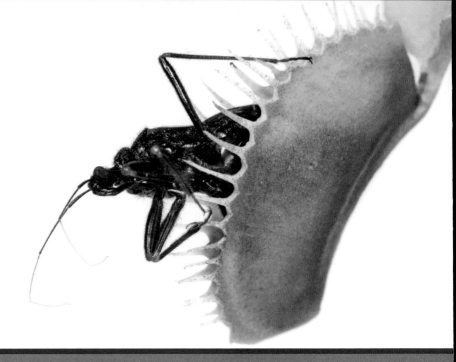

WORDS TO UNDERSTAND

carnivorous – a plant that is able to trap and then digest small animals, particularly insects

insectivorous – a plant that can capture and then digest insects

invertebrate – any animal that doesn't have a backbone or a spinal column, like insects, worms, snails, or jellyfish

mucilage – a liquid gummy secretion that is present in many carnivorous plants

photosynthesis – a process used by green plants and other organisms to convert energy from sunlight into chemical energy to grow

pseudobulb – a stem enlargement in many orchids, especially tropical orchids

CHAPTER 3

Trapping Plants

A plant that is **carnivorous** gets most of its nutrients from both trapping and then eating insects. It traps insects in 5 different ways:

1. Pitcher plants use a rolled leaf to make a pitfall trap. Insects will drop into a pool of bacteria or digestive enzymes;
2. Flypaper traps utilize a sticky, gluey substance called **mucilage**;
3. Bladder traps use a bladder that creates an internal vacuum to suck in prey
4. Snap traps use rapid leaf movements;
5. Eel traps, or lobster traps, force insects to move toward an awaiting digestive organ complete with inward pointing hairs.

Carnivorous or Litter Trapping Plants of Borneo

PITCHER PLANT (NEPENTHES) OR MONKEY CUPS

The two hundred forty different species of pitcher plants found in the Borneo rainforest have evolved a nice smelling, liquid-filled hollow section of their stems that attract insects and small mammals. The insects are lured by the smell and color of the plant into a cavity (which can be as tiny as a thimble, or large enough to hold half a gallon of liquid) where they then drown and are dissolved into the liquid. Larger pitcher plants have been known to drown a rat.

This beautiful plant is a distant cousin to North America's Venus flytrap. Some species have developed immunity

This pitcher plant contains a fluid with enzymes that digest insects that fall in.

Insects of Borneo beware...it's a trap.

Legend of the Man-Eating Tree

Explorers of the nineteenth-century jungles brought back outlandish tales of fabulous carnivorous plants that were large enough to capture and digest rodents like the mountain treeshrew and the summit rat. They told tales of the largest known pitcher plant trap, the Nepenthes rajah, which frequently has pitchers that are 16 inches (41 centimeters) tall and can hold 0.92 gallons (3.5 liters) of liquid. The reality is that it is rare that rodents find themselves falling into these large carnivorous pitchers.

Edmund Spencer wrote in an article for the April 26, 1874, issue of *New York World* that a German explorer named Karl Liche had witnessed a human sacrifice by Madagascar's Mkodo tribe. The legend tells of this tribe feeding a woman to a giant carnivorous plant, a demonic creature that strangled its prey by looping coils as big as serpents around her body and neck.

British author Phil Robinson repeated the tale of a man-eating tree in 1881 in his book *Under the Punkah*. He insisted that his "uncle" saw an "awful plant" that fed upon wild beasts and human slaves in a "Nubian fern forest."

The Bulbophyllum beccarii produces flowers that smell like rotting fish, attracting the flies it needs to help with pollination.

to the pitcher plant's poisons. Three examples are tree shrews (Tupaia montana), the common woolly bat, and a few nocturnal rats. The shrew will sit astride the pitcher plant's opening and lick the plant's nectar during the day; while it does so, it either urinates or defecates inside it, providing necessary nitrogen and phosphorus for the plant! The woolly bat actually sneaks into pitcher plants to sleep and defecate in it.

Pitcher plants actually grow two different kinds of pitchers for multi-use—a slippery, perfumed pitcher containing lots of digestive fluid that sprouts lower to the ground and is ideal for first catching and eating bugs; and a second pitcher that sprouts higher up and serves as a cozy little hotel room for shrews, rats, and bats.

LITTER-TRAPPING ORCHID OF SARAWAK, BORNEO

The magnificent Bulbophyllum beccarii is an orchid that grows upward by wrapping itself around tree trunks in the rainforests of Sarawak, Borneo. This orchid produces small, egg-shaped **pseudobulbs** that grow big, cup-shaped leaves. The "cup" part of this description is the most important. As debris and leaves fall from the tree canopy above, they are captured inside the cup. The orchid uses thousands of microbes and fungi to decompose the debris and feed itself.

Another strange feature of this plant is that, from time to time, it creates a dazzling clump of literally hundreds of teeny flowers. These flowers have a scent like rotting fish that is absolutely irresistible to carrion flies. These flies come looking for something to eat and a location to lay their eggs. They find nothing here, but the flies will rub up against the orchid pollen and transfer it elsewhere, which helps this orchid reproduce.

Utricularia Or Bladderworts

Utricularia, a carnivorous plant that uses a suction trap, can be found in tropical habitats around the world. Bladderworts trap insects inside a bladder functioning like a suction bulb. This bulb has tiny hair-like projections that are sensitive to the movement of passing insects, like water fleas. When the hairs are stimulated, the plant's flattened bladder immediately inflates, sucking in the passing insect and water at the same time. The bladder then closes an ingenious trap door after the insect is inside.

Some Utricularia are larger, and these plants also feed on mosquito larvae, fish fry (juvenile fish), and even young tadpoles. These ingenious plants thrive in tropical areas, freshwater marshes, and jungles.

Carnivorous Plants of The Amazon

BUTTERWORTS

Butterworts (Pinguicula) are carnivorous plants that use their sticky leaves to trap, lure, and digest insects. The greatest variety of species is found in the jungles of Central America and South America. These tropical butterworts form tight winter rosettes of fleshy leaves that are carnivorous all year round. These leaves are rigid, smooth, and succulent; they are usually an attractive pinkish or bright green color.

Butterworts have a sticky substance on their leaves that traps insects and digests all but the exoskeleton.

The butterwort has two specialized glands located on the upper leaf surface that secrete visible dewy-looking droplets that attract insects looking for water. Unfortunately for the insects, these droplets do not contain water. They are made up of a thick gluey substance that entraps the insects. The more the insects struggle, the more mucilage is created. Once the insect stops struggling, sessile glands start to release special proteins called enzymes that will digest the insect bodies. The plant leaves behind the exoskeleton of any larger insects on the surface of the leaf.

Insectivorous or Carnivorous Plants of The Democratic Republic of Congo (DRC)

GENLISEA OR CORKSCREW PLANTS

These plants grow well in the dripping swamps of the Central African jungle. They feature a small rosette of leaves that sit above the ground and carry out **photosynthesis**. They also have underground leaves that anchor the plant in place and serve to trap small **invertebrate** prey.

These leaves have a corkscrew-like, inverted Y-shape that attracts insects. Once inside the corkscrew, bristle-like hairs make sure that the prey cannot turn back and must keep going forward into the plant. When it reaches the digestive chamber of the plant, all of its nutrients are extracted.

Corkscrew plants trap small prey with underground leaves covered with bristle-like hairs.

Carnivorous Plants of Papua New Guinea

BYBLIS LINIFLORA

Byblis liniflora is a beautiful carnivorous plant that calls Papua New Guinea, Australia, and Indonesia its home. This species is sometimes called the rainbow plant because of its shimmering, dew-covered leaves. These leaves are thickly covered with glandular hairs that secrete a glue-like substance that ensnares small insects that get stuck in the sticky secretion. The insects that are too weak to get away will eventually suffocate or die of exhaustion.

It was thought for many years that plants of the Byblis species hosted live bugs that fed on the insects that were stuck and then nourished the plant with their feces. It was only in 2005 that it was proven that the plants themselves directly digested their insect prey with special enzymes, earning Byblis liniflora a rightful place among true carnivorous plants.

DROSERA BANKSII (BANKS' SUNDEW)

Banks' sundew is an annual plant with leaves arranged in a rosette around the stem and small white flowers. This

The appearance of dew on the leaves of the Byblis liniflora is one reason it is known as the rainbow plant. That dewy substance is really a glue-like secretion that traps small insects.

RESEARCH PROJECT

Take a look at the list of the 5 different ways that carnivorous plants capture their prey—pitfall traps, flypaper traps, snap traps, bladder traps, and lobster or eel traps. Choose one method and write a paper about several plants that use that particular method to capture insects.

Famous Flora

Probably the most famous carnivorous plant is the Venus flytrap. It has appeared in many movies and plays, especially one called *Little Shop of Horrors*. These plants have two matching padded leaves covered with thousands of tiny hairs. Whenever a fly or other insect touches any of those hairs, the Venus Flytrap snaps its leaves shut and starts releasing enzymes that will break down the fly in no time!

plant is one of between one hundred fifty-two and one hundred ninety-four species of Drosera. They are called sundews because of the small glue-filled drops atop their glandular hair that sparkle like dew when touched by sunlight.

The sundew traps its insect prey with its gluey hair and then rolls up its leaf edges. The insects die as the sweet-smelling glue (or mucilage) surrounds them, which usually takes about forty-five minutes. Once the prey is dead, this plant releases enzymes that cause the corpse to decompose and absorbs all the nutrients of its dead prey through its leaf surfaces.

Charles Darwin found this species of plant so fascinating that he completed many experiments with it and managed to fill up two hundred eighty-four pages in his book *Insectivorous Plants* with his experiments on it. Experiments studying sundews as a method of getting rid of insect pests in England estimated that a two-acre bog filled with sundew plants could eliminate six million insects at the same time!

The sticky hairs of the sundew trap insects drawn by its sweet scent.

TEXT-DEPENDENT QUESTIONS

1. What was the legend of the man-eating tree, and was this story true or false?
2. What scent is impossible to resist for carrion flies?
3. Does the butterwort plant consume the exoskeletons of larger insects?

WORDS TO UNDERSTAND

cardiorespiratory – relating to the action of the lungs and heart

centipede – a predatory invertebrate insect that has an elongated, flattened body consisting of many segments, each bearing one single pair of legs

initiation – a series of actions or a ceremony that allows a person to be formally accepted into an organization or group

larvae – an immature, active, wormlike, wingless form of an insect, that will eventually change into an adult through metamorphosis

CHAPTER 4

Deadly Bites

Amazon River Region

AMAZONIAN SPIDERS

There are an astounding three thousand six hundred different species of spiders calling the Amazon River basin their home, and many of them are deadly. Take the Brazilian wandering spider, for example. Eight species of this spider are venomous and highly aggressive. They are probably the most poisonous spiders on Earth, and one untreated bite is able to kill a human being in twenty-five minutes or less. These deadly critters frequently sneak into fruit that is being exported. A nickname for them is "banana spider" since they frequently hide in banana bunches and aren't discovered until they reach their destination.

AMAZONIAN GIANT CENTIPEDE

The Amazonian giant **centipede** (also called the Peruvian giant yellow-legged centipede), is a reddish, maroon-colored centipede boasting forty-six yellow-tinged legs that can grow as long as 12 inches. This is an extremely venomous and aggressive

The Amazonian giant centipede is not your average backyard creepy crawly. They are aggressive, venom-injecting hunters that can get to be as big as your forearm.

insect. They are the biggest centipedes in the world, commonly growing as long as a man's forearm. They are extremely fast runners and excellent climbers, and they use these skills at night when they go out on the prowl for prey.

Amazonian giant centipedes feed on practically anything they can kill, including bats, tarantulas, frogs, small lizards, mice, and sparrow-sized birds. With one rapid motion, this centipede snags onto its prey and injects a potent venom. Animals who get injected die after thrashing around for a few seconds. Their venom is toxic for humans too—a bite can cause chills, fatigue, severe pain, and swelling.

This monster centipede catches bats by scaling cave walls to reach the ceiling, where it hangs down and lets its forward segments wriggle freely in the air to snatch onto an unsuspecting victim in mid-flight. A bat will attempt to get away from the deadly grasp of centipede legs but will not succeed because the poison kills it within a matter of seconds. After the bat's death, the giant centipede will leisurely dangle from the ceiling of the cave while eating every piece of flesh from its prey in about an hour. After this hour-long gorge, the centipede then scurries back down the cave wall and returns to its lair to sleep off its gigantic meal.

BRAZILIAN YELLOW SCORPION

The Brazilian yellow scorpion (Tityus serrulatus), a resident of the tropical rainforest as well as more urban areas of Brazil, is currently considered to be the deadliest scorpion in the South America. The venom of this scorpion contains a powerful poison. If a human receives a small-to-moderately sized bite, they can suffer from nausea, sweating, fever, cramps, vomiting, and localized pain. A bigger bite can be

The Brazilian yellow scorpion is the deadliest scorpion in South America.

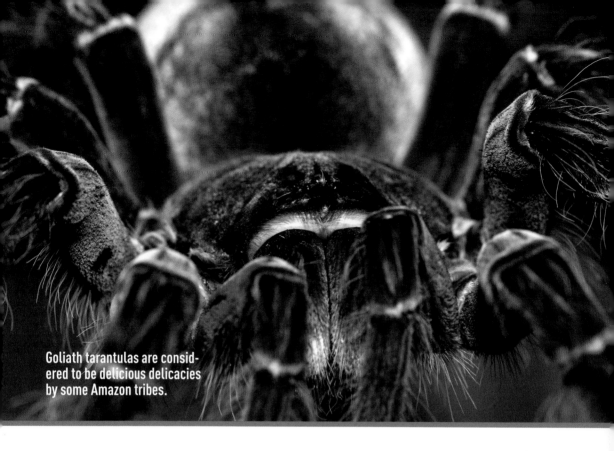

Goliath tarantulas are considered to be delicious delicacies by some Amazon tribes.

lethal for elderly people and children since it can result in **cardiorespiratory** failure. This scorpion is estimated to sting over a million people each year! These deadly brownish-yellow scorpions are relatively small in size and reproduce asexually, which allows their population to grow at a rapid rate. They can birth nineteen to twenty offspring at one time.

THE GOLIATH BIRD-EATING TARANTULA OF SOUTH AMERICA

Imagine being in the Amazon Jungle and coming across a spider that is as large as a young puppy! Its feet have claws or hardened tips that make a distinct, clicking sound. Additionally, prickly hairs with microscopic barbs cover this scary creature, and it has two fangs that can grow to be 1 1/2 inches (3.8 centimeters) long. This monster's bite is venomous and extremely painful, but fortunately, it is not deadly to humans. The Piaroa tribe of Venezuela eats these spiders and considers them a great delicacy. They are roasted, and their fangs are served on the side to be used as toothpicks!

BULLET ANTS

Bullet ants, also known as conga ants, were given their name after gaining a reputation

Flannel Moth Caterpillars of Central America

These insects look like small, innocent, fluffy moths, but they are feared for their stinging ability. They are covered with yellow, gray, or red hairs called setae and look harmless; but beware—if their spines touch your skin, you will experience headaches, vomiting, and pain.

The bite of a bullet ant is notoriously painful.

for having a sting that hurts like a gunshot! The Sateré-Mawe people, an indigenous tribe of Amazonia, Brazil, has an **initiation** rite for boys who want to become warriors. They must put on gloves that are filled with bullet ants and keep them on for ten minutes; and not just once, but many times!

The Truth About Bullet Ants

Bullet ants will attack with one of the most painful stings in the world...unless you're nice to them.

Sarawak, Borneo

CENTIPEDES OF BORNEO

Centipedes are common in the jungles of Borneo. These are predators that prowl at night, mostly hunting other invertebrates. Some of the larger species are able to inflict painful bites. The Bornean cave centipede is known locally as "the creature from the darkest corner of Hell." This fast-moving, long-legged, brownish-red centipede with light brown striped legs and large antennae hangs out on cave walls, hates any light, and will not hesitate to give you a nasty bite if you happen to enter its territory.

STINGING ARMY ANTS OF BORNEO

These swarming insects form gigantic raiding storms and are known to attack whatever creature, living or dead, that they cross. They will even carry away the leftovers from your dinner! Birds can get overwhelmed by thousands of stings and are cut apart alive, and the pieces are carried back to the nests of these stinging army ants. These ants are nocturnal, entering hen houses and killing sleeping chickens, for example. Villagers with houses close to the jungle's edge will lock up their chickens at night. In the morning, they will enter the chicken coop, only to discover that all that remains are a few chicken heads, some feathers, and a few bones!

At the edge of the jungle in Borneo, swarms of army ants have been known to wipe out an entire chicken coop overnight.

Asian Giant Hornets

Asian giant hornets are the apex predator of the insect kingdom in Central China, Japan, Korea, Vietnam, Thailand, Nepal, and India. These large brown and yellow-orange hornets are the largest hornets in the world. They live in low-altitude forests and possess a one-inch-long (10 millimeter) stinger, filled with a potent venom that is capable of killing a human being (in combination with other giant hornet stings). One lucky person who survived a giant hornet attack said that its sting felt "like a hot nail being driven into my leg."

About twenty people die from their stings in Japan every year. Death occurs by cardiac arrest or from multiple organ failures. The average number of stings it takes to kill an individual is fifty-nine. These hornets prey on other hornet colonies and honeybee hives. One Asian giant hornet is able to kill approximately twenty bees each minute because of its large jaws (or mandibles), which they use to decapitate their prey.

The Asian giant hornet is the largest hornet in the world.

African Biting Insects of The Central and West African Jungles

AFRICAN EYEWORMS

The loa loa (or African eyeworm) transmits disease throughout the jungles of Western and Central Africa via repetitive bites of the mango fly. This fly has infected **larvae** in its mouth that enter through the wound in the skin left by these flies. It takes five months for the larvae to transform into adult worms that can live between the layers of your skin. If a female loa loa is fertilized, she can produce thousands of larvae daily. These larvae travel through your bloodstream and accumulate in your lungs!

RESEARCH PROJECT

Study all of the deadly biting and stinging insects discussed in this chapter. What might happen if these insects were pitted against one another? Which insect species would be declared the deadliest in a competition of this type? Compare and contrast them in a chart, using images to illustrate as needed.

These particular larvae create Calabar swellings, which are itching body swellings found near joints or on limbs. They can also cause an eye worm to literally crawl across your eye surface and cause itching, pain, eye congestion, and light sensitivity. The worst part is that these parasites can live in your system for seventeen years unless they are surgically removed! Humans who want to avoid getting bit should stay away from any shaded, muddy areas along the river in these jungles.

Papua New Guinea

CENTIPEDES OF PAPUA NEW GUINEA

Centipede bites are common in some regions of Papua New Guinea. Reactions to the bite of this insect, which can reach a length of 11.8 inches (30 centimeters), may include severe swelling, itching, pain, fever, nausea, blistering, and shortness of breath. Centipede bites are considered especially dangerous for children and the elderly.

MARBLED SCORPIONS

This species, also known as little marbled bark scorpion, can be found in the wet coastal eucalyptus jungles of Papua New Guinea. They live high up in trees under the bark, among leaf litter on jungle floors, and underneath the bark of fallen logs. These scorpions have a reputation for being among the most venomous scorpion species found on Earth, but significant testing has not been carried out. Bites of the marbled scorpion cause numbness, severe pain, redness, and swelling.

The legs of the Amazonian Giant Centipede can each grow to be a foot long.

TEXT-DEPENDENT QUESTIONS

1. What is the largest centipede in the world?
2. Name the ways that the larvae of the loa loa can affect the human body.
3. What deadly insects are part of an initiation ritual of the Sateré-Mawe people?

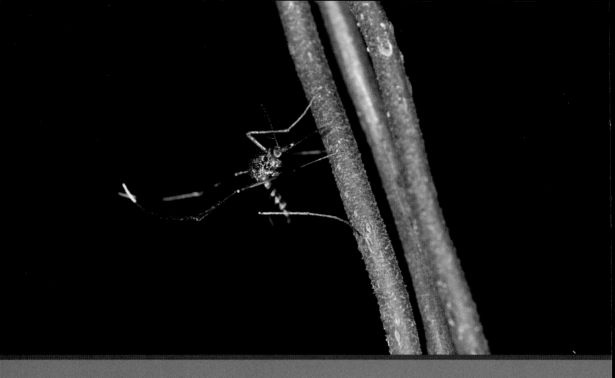

WORDS TO UNDERSTAND

acrid – sharp, bitterly pungent smell or taste that can be irritating to the nose, eyes, etc.

invasive – something that tends to spread profusely, harmfully, and undesirably

mandible – the lower jaw of some insects that are equipped to bite or crush their prey

parasites – organisms that live in or on an organism from another species, called the host, from which it obtains nutrients

protozoan – a microscopic single-celled animal such as a flagellate, amoeba, sporozoan, or ciliate

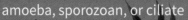

CHAPTER 5

Airborne Attacks

Flying Insects of The Amazon Rainforest

Flying insects are truly the masters of their environment in the jungle. They navigate easily through trees and lush plants to find water, food, companionship, and prey.

TITAN BEETLE (TITANUS GIGANTEUS)

The titan beetle is the largest species of longhorn beetle to call the Amazon River basin home. They are able to grow up to 6.6 inches (16.76 meters) long! These insects fly through the jungle or wander around the jungle floor in search of prey. Because their first set of wings transforms into a sort of protective casing, titan beetles are more skilled in roaming the floor like protected tanks and are less skilled in flying, where they are prone to accidents.

These monsters don't care when they crash—they simply emit a loud hissing sound and get back on their way. Titan beetles can snap pencils in half with their **mandibles**, and there are reports that they are able to rip into human flesh with equal ferociousness! Adult titan beetles defend themselves by biting and hissing a warning, and these critters have sharp spines in addition to their strong jaws.

MOSQUITOES

The Amazon River basin is a perfect breeding ground for all types of mosquitoes—they thrive in warm, humid environments. Scientists estimate that there are approximately three thousand one hundred different mosquito species in the jungle. An interesting fact is that male mosquitoes don't bite! They only eat nectar. It's the female mosquitoes that suck vertebrate blood (blood from any animal that has a spinal column or a backbone) to help their eggs develop.

Female mosquitoes usually rest during the day and start flying at sundown. They lay their eggs in water, so they are typically found close to swamps and rivers. The main diseases that these mosquitoes carry are malaria, dengue fever, and yellow fever. Because of this fact, mosquitoes are considered the greatest threat to humans traveling or living in the Amazon region.

Pregnancy Cravings

In the jungles of Belize, there lives a bloodthirsty insect called the botlass fly. The strongest insect repellants in the world are no match for these insects. They bite twenty-four hours a day, using their strong jaws with sharp serrated edges to sever tiny blood vessels and slash through flesh. As soon as a wound is created, the botlass fly is lapping it up. Like most bloodsucking species, it is only the female who has bloodlust because blood has the protein source she needs for growing upwards of eight hundred eggs during her lifetime.

A massive hive of African honey bees filling the canopy of a tree.

Indigenous tribespeople know a trick to cope with these constantly biting insects—they never scratch. If you don't scratch a bite, it doesn't itch as much. Visitors to the Amazon region must get a full set of vaccinations before entering the jungle. While you are there, drink only bottled water, use mosquito repellent lavishly, and sleep under mosquito netting. It's no joke that the diseases these mosquitoes carry can kill you!

AFRICANIZED HONEY BEES

These bees are native to Africa but are now most frequently found in the rainforests of South America. The rainforest tribes fear them because they kill by swarming and stinging their prey. These bees are known for being the most aggressive bees in the world. It is said that once one bee decides to attack, the whole hive will swarm; and they have been known to chase possible victims for more than half a mile!

ASSASSIN FLIES

These carnivorous flies of the Amazon rainforest are predators of bees and other insects. Their secret weapon is poisonous saliva, and they use this saliva to bring down wasps, bees, spiders, dragonflies, beetles, and other flies. These aggressive insects perch on rocks and vegetation to watch for any insects flying by. Once they spot their prey, they follow it and attack it mid-flight by grabbing it with its legs, biting it on its side or back, and injecting its venomous saliva. Assassin bugs are so ingenious that they sometimes cover themselves with ant carcasses so they will smell like a nonthreatening ant to their deceived prey. Sometimes, they also cover themselves with leaf debris so that they look just like a harmless pile of rubbish. When their victim passes by, they fly out and attack their prey.

The poison kills insects almost instantly and actually liquefies its insides so the assassin fly can suck its insides out

An assassin fly takes on a goldenrod crab spider.

using its specially adapted mouthparts. Once their prey is dead, the assassin fly will make a basket out of its bristly, strong legs to carry the prey to a safe place so the fly can devour its prey at its leisure.

STINGLESS BEES

There is a species of stingless bees that live in the Amazon River basin. Although their stingers are quite tiny, they can do other nasty things if they are disturbed. Although a few species attempt to fly into your ears and mouth to make you get out of their area, other species can bite, cut your skin, and spray a nasty **acrid** solution out of their mandibles into the wound, causing painful blisters. No wonder they are also called fire bees!

Stingless bees like to live close to jungle villages, where they hang out close to garbage piles, food leftovers, or on top of human excrement. Villagers know that there is an important relationship between these bees and the jungle plants and trees that surround them, so they learn to live with them, making sure to avoid as much as possible their bites and stinging sprays.

RESEARCH PROJECT

Many of the flying insects covered in this chapter transmit diseases. Choose 3 different diseases that are spread by these flying insects and compare and contrast them. Write a paper discussing the diseases you have selected, and discuss which insects carry the disease, and how they infect human beings.

African Rainforest Flying Insects

TSETSE FLIES OF THE CONGO RIVER BASIN

Deep in the Congo River basin exist thousands upon thousands of tsetse flies, which look similar to horse flies and have a fifty percent or greater chance of carrying sleeping sickness (African trypanosomiasis). It only takes one painful bite from a gray-brown honey-bee-sized tsetse fly to infect a human with **parasites** in their blood. Symptoms can take months or sometimes even years to appear after a person is bitten.

The first symptoms associated with sleeping sickness are severe muscle aches, headaches, high fevers, face swelling, weight loss, and swollen lymph nodes. These symptoms may be followed by confusion, sleep disturbances, poor coordination, and behavior changes. If this disease goes untreated, the infection is usually fatal within one or two years.

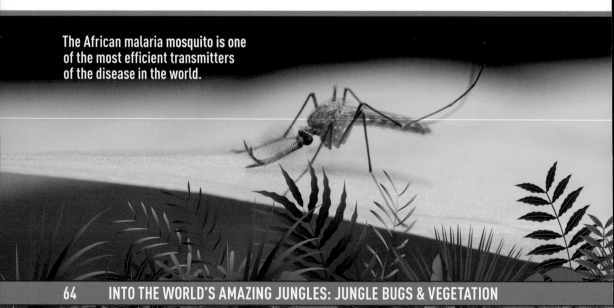

The African malaria mosquito is one of the most efficient transmitters of the disease in the world.

AFRICAN MOSQUITO (ANOPHELES GAMBIAE)

The African mosquito (Anopheles gambiae) is so good at transmitting malaria that it's frequently called simply the African malaria mosquito. This flying pest is found throughout the jungle, and funnily enough is attracted to warm skin, particularly foot odor caused by bacteria in sweat. Their population increases during the rainy season. The disease is rampant, but treatable. In 2010, there were five hundred ninety-six thousand deaths out of one hundred seventy-four million malaria cases in Africa, well under one percent.

It's important to know that the mosquito doesn't cause malaria. A **protozoan** parasite is transmitted by the female mosquito's saliva when she feeds on blood. Anopheles gambiae inhabit shallow temporary pools or puddles of sunlit fresh water, including small ground depressions or even a small amount of water in a hoof print. The larvae of this insect develops in only six days—that's just six days to transform from an egg into an adult! The female mosquitoes hunt at night, and they are known to be the most successful malaria transmitters in the world!

Binge Eating

Farmers throughout the world are subjected every so often to invading swarms of voracious insects. Occasionally gigantic swarms of insects will change their typical behavior and migrate to areas of heavy plant growth, where they will then eat everything in sight. Locusts are particularly known for this type of behavior. A swarm of one square kilometer that is made up of forty million locusts can eat the exact same amount in one day as approximately thirty-five thousand people!

A wasp perches on a leaf in the jungle of Papua New Guinea.

Flying Attacking Insects of Papua New Guinea

VESPIDAE WASPS OR HORNETS

Most of the wasps that can be found in the jungles of Papua New Guinea are solitary and present no hazard to human beings. However, case studies exist that tell of vicious attacks by colonies of large Vespidae wasps (commonly known there as hornets) that have resulted in deaths or acute kidney failure. Surviving victims were hospitalized for multiple wasp stings.

Like all hornets throughout the world, the wasps of Papua New Guinea like to nest close to where human beings live, and they are fierce protectors of their nesting sites. Hornet stings are much more painful than bee stings or stings by smaller species of wasps. They can sting repeatedly and unlike their relative, the honey bee, they don't die after they sting because hornet stingers aren't barbed and don't get pulled out of the hornet's body.

Hornets also have a scary habit of mobilizing their entire nest to sting defensively, which is dangerous both for humans and other animals. If someone kills a hornet close to their nest it can release pheromones (chemical substances that are produced and released into the air by an insect which can affect the behavior of other insects of its species) that alert the nest to mobilize.

The wasps of Papua New Guinea also attack other insects, killing them with stings and with their jaws. Because of their larger size, they can kill honey bees, locusts, and grasshoppers easily. The dead prey is then completely chewed up and fed to all the larvae growing inside the wasp nest.

Garuda Warrior Wasp

A previously unknown warrior wasp (named garuda) was discovered in 2011 on Sulawesi in Indonesia. This wasp, which is about 2 1/2 inches (6.35 centimeters) long, has been nicknamed the Komodo dragon of wasps since it delivers an extremely vicious sting using jaws that are longer than its own front legs! The warrior wasp has gigantic ninja-like mandibles.

The Flying Bloodsuckers of Borneo

ASIAN TIGER MOSQUITOES

Although the rainforests of Borneo are rapidly disappearing, there are still areas where animals abound and ravenous swarms of mosquitoes roam the jungle. There are recent cases of human beings caught and bitten by huge swarms of Asian tiger mosquitoes (Aedes aegypti), the species of mosquito that is primarily responsible for spreading dengue fever, yellow fever, West Nile Fever, the deadly Zika virus, and sixteen other diseases throughout the world.

How Mosquitoes Use Six Needles to Suck Your Blood | Deep Look

Mosquitos at work...watch them do their thing.

The Asian tiger mosquito is smart, resilient, has an aggressive nature and an increasing desire for human blood. Although it thrives in the jungle, it also can live in urban environments and more temperate climates. This monster bites all day—unlike the majority of other species of mosquitos that tend to bite only at dawn and at dusk. It also eats quickly—it alights on its victim's skin for just a few seconds, as opposed to other mosquito species that stay on your skin and drink their fill, making it much easier for the victim to swat them away or kill them.

There is a special list, compiled by the Global Invasive Species Database, entitled the "World's One Hundred Worst Invasive Alien Species," and the Asian tiger mosquito is one of the few insect species to make the list.

The Asian tiger mosquito is instantly recognizable by its distinctive black-and-white-striped markings.

TEXT-DEPENDENT QUESTIONS

1. How large can a titan beetle get?
2. Which African insect is known to carry the sleeping sickness disease?
3. Name three diseases carried by the Asian tiger mosquito.

SERIES GLOSSARY OF KEY TERMS

Assimilation - the process by which a person or persons acquire the social and psychological characteristics of a group or society

Canopy - also called crown canopy or crown cover, this refers to the cover formed by the leafy upper branches of the trees in a forest

Carnivorous - subsisting or feeding on animal tissues, or in the case of some plants, subsisting on nutrients obtained from the breakdown of animal protoplasm

Colonialism - control by one country over another area and its people

Conservation - a careful preservation and protection of something, such as the planned management of a natural resource to prevent exploitation, destruction, or neglect

Creature – an animal of any type

Culture – the customary beliefs, social forms, and material traits of a racial, religious, or social group, and the characteristic features of everyday existence (such as diversions or a way of life) shared by the people of those groups in a place or time

Deforestation – the action or process of the clearing of forests through cutting or burning its trees

Enzymes - any of numerous complex proteins that are produced by living cells and catalyze specific natural biochemical reactions at body temperatures, such as digestion

Habitat - the place or environment where a plant or animal naturally or normally lives and grows

Indigenous - produced, growing, living, or occurring naturally in a particular region or environment

Nocturnal - active at night

Oxygen - a reactive element that is found in water, in most rocks and minerals, in numerous organic compounds, and as a colorless tasteless odorless diatomic gas constituting 21 percent of the atmosphere, that is capable of combining with all elements except the inert gases and is active in physiological processes. Estimates say that trees of the world's jungles produce 30 to 55 percent of the oxygen in the atmosphere

Parasite - an animal, insect or plant that lives in or on another animal or plant and gets food or protection from it

Poaching – to trespass on land for the purpose of taking fish or game illegally

Predator - an animal that lives by killing and eating other animals

Rainforest - a tropical woodland with an annual rainfall of at least 100 inches (254 centimeters) and marked by lofty broad-leaved evergreen trees forming a continuous canopy

Species - a category of biological classification ranking immediately below the genus or subgenus, comprising related organisms or populations potentially capable of interbreeding, and being designated by a common name

Tropical - of, being, or characteristic of a region or climate that is frost-free with temperatures high enough to support year-round plant growth given sufficient moisture

Venom - a toxic substance produced by some animals (such as snakes, scorpions, or bees) that is injected into prey or an enemy chiefly by biting or stinging and has an injurious or lethal effect

The Jungle of the Red Spirit, 2012

The jungles of Borneo are especially famous for the enormous number of species of the most sophisticated flower in the world—the Orchid. In this documentary, viewers will see the beauty close-up as they climb the tree trunks of this beautiful jungle guided by the "man of the forest."

The Sacred Science, 2011

In October of 2010, eight people, suffering from various illnesses, chose to leave everything behind and spend thirty days in a corner of the world that is home to a vanishing group of indigenous healers in uncharted regions of the Amazon rainforest. Five would come back with real results, two would come back disappointed, and one wouldn't come back at all. This is their story.

Swamp Tigers, 2001

This documentary takes a look at one of the most efficient predators on Earth. Cameraman Mike Herd captured the legendary swamp tiger on film for the first time years ago. It was an extraordinary breakthrough, the first glimpse into the secret life of the least known tiger in the world - the swamp tiger of the Bangladeshi Sundarbans.

RESOURCES

FURTHER READING

Clarkson, Tommy, And Patty. *The Civilized Jungle: Tropical Plants Facts and Fun From Ola Brisa Gardens* (Volume 1). Manzanillo, Mexico: Tommy Clarkson, 2016.

Hondo, Makoto. *Carnivorous Plants in The Wilderness: Color Photo Edition*. Charleston: CreateSpace Independent Publishing Platform, 2013.

Purser, Bruce. *Jungle Bugs: Masters of Camouflage And Mimicry*. Ontario: Firefly Books, 2003.

Schmidt, Justin O. *The Sting of The Wild*. Baltimore: Johns Hopkins University Press, 2016.

Spielman, Andrew. Mosquito: *The Story of Man's Deadliest Foe*. New York: Hachette Books, 2002.

Tornio, Stacy. *Plants That Can Kill: 101 Toxic Species to Make You Think Twice*. New York: Skyhorse Publishing, 2017.

Walters, Martin. *The Illustrated World Encyclopedia of Insects: A Natural History And Identification Guide to Beetles, Flies, Bees, Wasps, Springtails, Mayflies…Crickets, Bugs, Grasshoppers, Fleas, Spiders*. Armadillo, TX: Lorenz Books, Anness Publishing Company, 2011.

INTERNET RESOURCES

http://www.npr.org/sections/thetwo-way/2017/02/06/513315490/carnivorous-plants-around-the-globe-use-similar-deadly-tricks
Breaking news from NPR features a podcast from *All Things Considered* and some interesting information on carnivorous plants around the world.

http://wwf.panda.org/what_we_do/where_we_work/borneo_forests/about_borneo_forests/borneo_animals/borneo_plants/
World Wildlife Federation (WWF) discusses the tropical vegetation of Borneo's rainforest.

http://mrmedizin.com/forum/rainforest-plants
This page gathers together interesting facts and videos about the rainforest, created by David Attenborough for BBC Wildlife and other quality sources.

http://www.worldatlas.com/articles/threatened-native-plants-of-papua-new-guinea.html
This webpage was created by WorldAtlas and provides interesting information about threatened native plants of Papua New Guinea.

http://globalforestatlas.yale.edu/amazon/ecoregions/ecology-amazon-rainforest
This interesting site on Amazon forest ecology was created by the Yale School of Forestry & Environmental Studies Global Forest Atlas.

EDUCATIONAL VIDEO LINKS:

Chapter 1: http://x-qr.net/1DCt

CAPTION: The public is invited to the smelly experience that is the corpse flower at the US Botanic Garden in Washington, D.C.

Chapter 2: http://x-qr.net/1Ht0

CAPTION: Learn about the dangers of the Giant Stinging Tree.

Chapter 3: http://x-qr.net/1Eg1

CAPTION: Insects of Borneo beware…it's a trap.

Chapter 4: http://x-qr.net/1Hkf

CAPTION: Watch a westerner take a tribal initiation challenge…and fail.

Chapter 5: http://x-qr.net/1D2o

CAPTION: Mosquitos at work…watch them do their thing.

INDEX

ABOUT THE AUTHOR

Lori is a graduate of the University of Pittsburgh and has traveled all over Central and South America. She loves books, learning, music, traveling, and new opportunities. Since an early age, she has written articles for newspapers and magazines. For more than a decade, she has been an editorial and design judge for the Benjamin Franklin Publishing Awards. As a cataloger in a large university library, she created thousands of bibliographic records detailing content and subject headings of books. She is also a prolific blogger known for her thoughtful writing, as well as her keen sense of humor. To top it all off, Lori is fluent in Spanish.

Photo credits: Chapter 1 - © Kidsada Manchinda | Dreamstime; © Kseniya Ragozina | Dreamstime; © Paulgrecaud | Dreamstime; © Derek Garcia | Dreamstime; © Oliver Sepp | Dreamstime; © Irina Chicherova | Dreamstime; © Pipa100 | Dreamstime; Chapter 2 - © Kerry Hill | Dreamstime; © Ammit | Dreamstime; © Woravit Vijitpanya | Dreamstime; © Rozenn Leard | Dreamstime; Milky Mangrove © Dinesh Valke from Thane, India | Wikicommons; Pangium edule seeds © Midori | Wikicommons; © Baoshengrulai | Dreamstime; © Lungsua | Dreamstime; Chapter 3 - © Micca44 | Dreamstime; © Paul Cowan | Dreamstime; © Shelagh Duffett | Dreamstime; © Johannes Hansen | Dreamstime; Genlisea © Denis Barthel | Wikicommons; © Alexander Fisch | Wikicommons; © Merkushev | Dreamstime; © Nicku | Dreamstime; Chapter 4 - © Pablo Hidalgo | Dreamstime; © Tod Baker from Tianjin, China | Wikicommons; © Claudio Pedroso | Dreamstime; © Spaceheater | Dreamstime; © Pablo Hidalgo | Dreamstime; © Romangorielov | Dreamstime; © Feathercollector | Dreamstime; Chapter 5 - © Asdf_1 | Dreamstime; © Paula French | Dreamstime; © Aleoks | Dreamstime; © Dykyostudio | Dreamstime; © Isaac Mcevoy | Dreamstime; © Itsik Marom | Dreamstime